THIS PLANNER
Belongs To:

THOUGHTS *Tracker*

MONITORING YOUR THOUGHTS & FEELINGS

MONDAY'S THOUGHTS

TUESDAY'S THOUGHTS

WEDNESDAY'S THOUGHTS

THURSDAY'S THOUGHTS

FRIDAY'S THOUGHTS

SATURDAY'S THOUGHTS

SUNDAY'S THOUGHTS

TRANSFORMING *Thoughts*

TRANSFORMING NEGATIVE THOUGHTS

We all deal with negative thoughts and self-doubt. Use this space to keep track of those feelings and focus on how you can replace them with positive thoughts that promote self-growth.

NEGATIVE THOUGHT	REPLACEMENT THOUGHT
NEGATIVE THOUGHT	REPLACEMENT THOUGHT
NEGATIVE THOUGHT	REPLACEMENT THOUGHT
NEGATIVE THOUGHT	REPLACEMENT THOUGHT
NEGATIVE THOUGHT	REPLACEMENT THOUGHT
NEGATIVE THOUGHT	REPLACEMENT THOUGHT

PERSONAL REFLECTIONS

SELF AWARENESS *Chart*

CHALLENGE NEGATIVE THOUGHTS AND FEELINGS

It's easy to get lost in our own headspace so it's important that you question any negative feelings so you can sort through your emotions effectively. Use this worksheet to document your progress.

THOUGHT

IS THE THOUGHT VALID?

HOW DO YOU REACT TO THIS NEGATIVE THOUGHT?

WHAT COULD YOU DO TO AVOID FEELING THIS WAY?

THOUGHTS & REFLECTIONS

MOOD *Chart*

Use the wheel below to document your moods every month.
Use 3 different colors to represent positive, negative or neutral emotions.

☐ POSITIVE ☐ NEGATIVE ☐ NEUTRAL

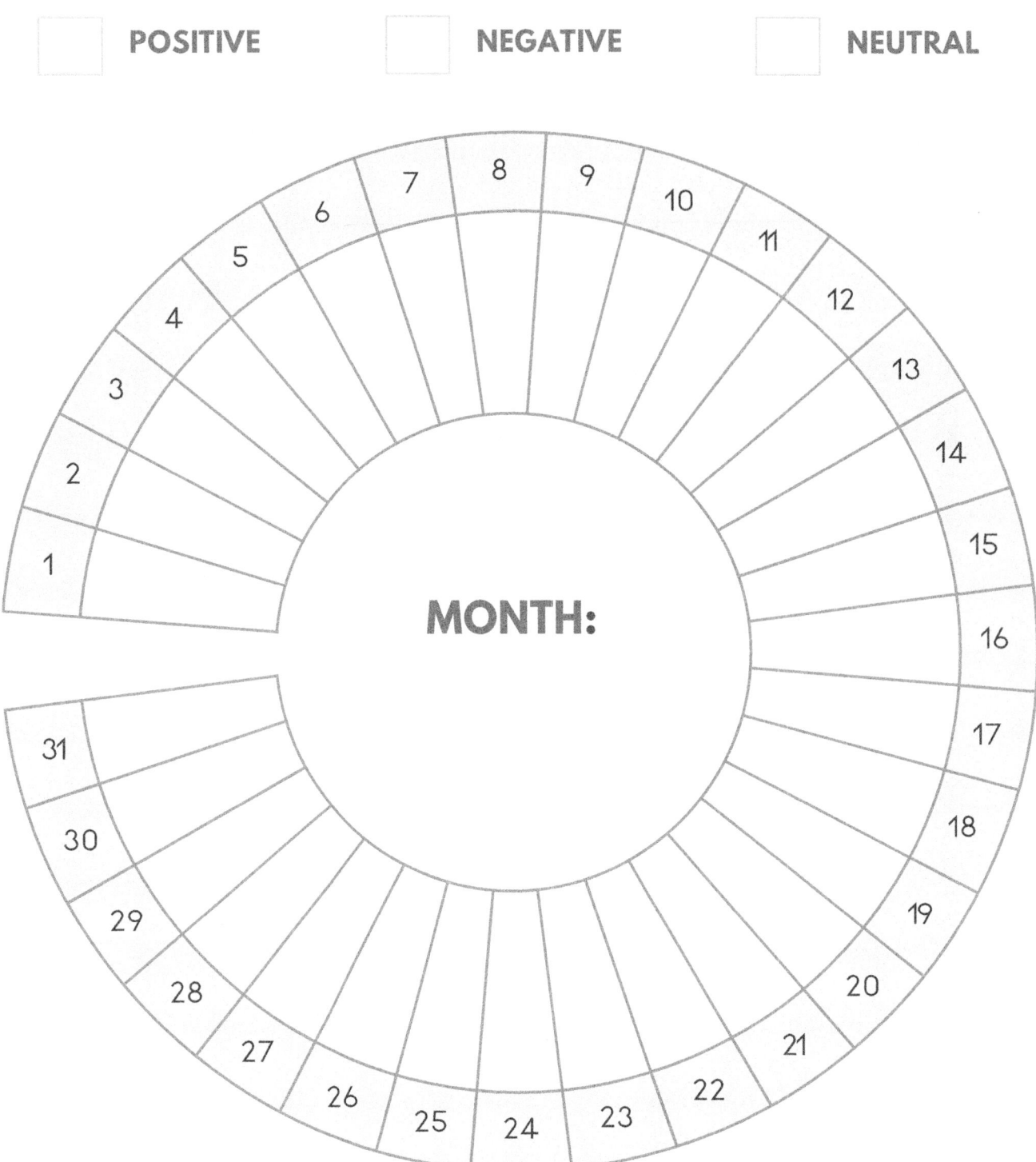

SLEEP Tracker

MONTH: _____

Sleep plays a major factor in our ability to cope with anxiety and depression. Keep track of your sleep pattern in order to determine how the amount of rest may be affecting your mental health.

DAY	HOURS SLEPT	QUALITY OF SLEEP	THOUGHTS
1			
2			
3			
4			
5			
6			
7			
8			
9			
10			
11			
12			
13			
14			
15			
16			
17			
18			
19			
20			
21			
22			
23			
24			
25			
26			
27			
28			
29			
30			
31			

LIFE *Assessment*

SUMMARIZE HOW YOU FEEL ABOUT YOUR LIFE

TOP 3 AREAS OF YOUR LIFE YOU'D LIKE TO IMPROVE

01

02

03

3 WAYS YOU CAN ACCOMPLISH YOUR LIFE GOALS

MONTH: _____

TRIGGER *Tracker*

Keep track of experiences that generate negative thoughts and emotions.

DATE	INCIDENT	REACTION

GRATEFUL *Heart*

MONTH: _____

DAY | TODAY I AM GRATEFUL FOR:

1
2
3
4
5
6
7
8
9
10
11
12
13
14
15
16
17
18
19
20
21
22
23
24
25
26
27
28
29
30
31

SELF Improvement

WHAT ARE YOUR SELF SABOTAGE HABITS?

Eliminate Negative Habits | **Create Positive Habits**

HOW CAN YOU IMPROVE YOUR MENTAL HEALTH?

What Key Areas Need Work? | **What Are Some Steps You Can Take?**

ANALYZING THE PEOPLE IN YOUR LIFE

Who Are The Negative Influences? | **Who Are The Positive Influences?**

HOW DO I HOLD MYSELF ACCOUNTABLE?

What I Know I'm Responsible For | **Who Helps Keep Me Accountable?**

SELF CARE *Ideas*

NURTURE YOUR MIND

Discover new hobbies
Read a book
Take a road trip
Keep a journal
Talk to a friend

Follow inspiring people
Challenge yourself
Be grateful
Call an old friend
Try something new

FEED YOUR SPIRIT

Have "me-time"
Listen to music
Read poetry
Write "future-self"
Paint
Meditate

TAKE CARE OF YOUR BODY

Eat healthy
Start a workout plan
Get enough sleep
Stay hydrated
Yoga

Ideas

SELF CARE *Planner*

Self-care involves taking care of yourself emotionally, mentally and physically.
Create a self-care plan by adding activities to the categories below.

MENTAL SELF-CARE	PHYSICAL SELF-CARE (GET ACTIVE)

EMOTIONAL SELF-CARE	DAILY HABITS (SLEEP, ETC.)

REACH OUT (SOCIALIZE)	SUPPORT NETWORK

OTHER:

SELF CARE Tracker

Self care is an important step in managing anxiety and depression. It helps us recharge, reset and nurtures our mind and soul. Focus on incorporating one self-care activity into your daily life.

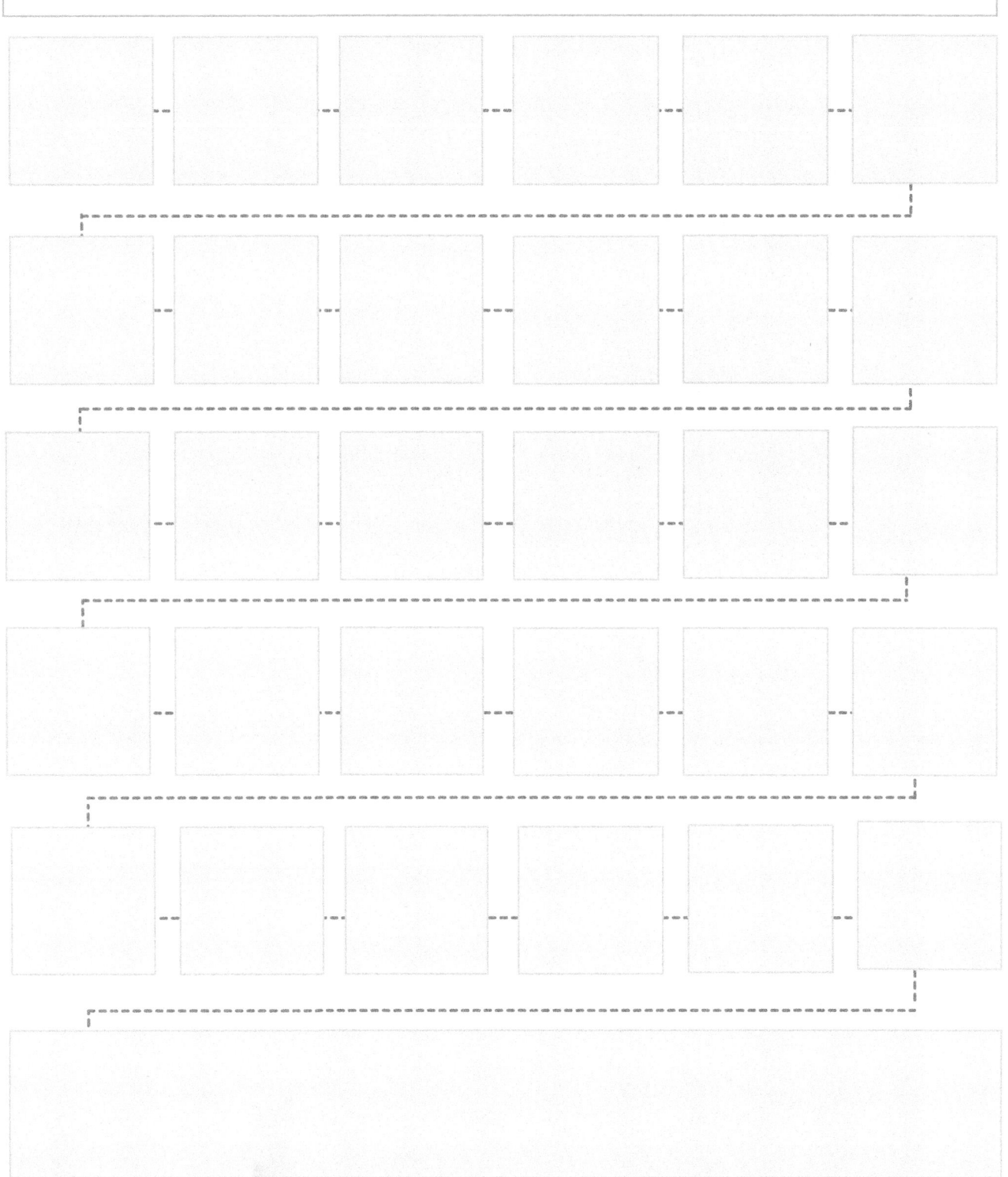

MONTH: _____

THOUGHT *Log*

Keep track of negative thoughts so you can learn how to control irrational responses and triggers.

DATE	INCIDENT	INITIAL REACTION	RATIONAL REACTION

PERSONAL Wins

MONTH:

It's important to celebrate both minor and major wins when it comes to your mental health and the coping strategies you've learned along the way. You've come a long way!

2 RECENT WINS

TOP 3 MILESTONES

1.
2.
3.

3 THINGS I'VE LEARNED ABOUT MYSELF OVER THE LAST YEAR

PERSONAL REFLECTIONS	HOW I'VE LEARNED TO COPE WITH EMOTIONS

NOTES

PERSONAL *Rewards*

MONTH:

Make sure to reward yourself for accomplishments throughout your journey. Whether it's a visit to your favorite restaurant, a bubble bath or an evening with friends, it's important to celebrate your progress every step of the way.

IDEAS FOR PERSONAL REWARDS

1	2
3	4
5	6

HOW I FELT BEFORE	HOW I REWARDED MYSELF	HOW I FELT AFTER REWARD

NOTES	PERSONAL REFLECTIONS/THOUGHTS

ANXIETY Tracker

Document the days when you experienced anxiety. This page includes a 3-week tracker.

ANXIETY LEVELS (1-MILD, 10 SEVERE)

Day												
MON	01	02	03	04	05	06	07	08	09	10	11	12
TUE	01	02	03	04	05	06	07	08	09	10	11	12
WED	01	02	03	04	05	06	07	08	09	10	11	12
THU	01	02	03	04	05	06	07	08	09	10	11	12
FRI	01	02	03	04	05	06	07	08	09	10	11	12
SAT	01	02	03	04	05	06	07	08	09	10	11	12
SUN	01	02	03	04	05	06	07	08	09	10	11	12
MON	01	02	03	04	05	06	07	08	09	10	11	12
TUE	01	02	03	04	05	06	07	08	09	10	11	12
WED	01	02	03	04	05	06	07	08	09	10	11	12
THU	01	02	03	04	05	06	07	08	09	10	11	12
FRI	01	02	03	04	05	06	07	08	09	10	11	12
SAT	01	02	03	04	05	06	07	08	09	10	11	12
SUN	01	02	03	04	05	06	07	08	09	10	11	12
MON	01	02	03	04	05	06	07	08	09	10	11	12
TUE	01	02	03	04	05	06	07	08	09	10	11	12
WED	01	02	03	04	05	06	07	08	09	10	11	12
THU	01	02	03	04	05	06	07	08	09	10	11	12
FRI	01	02	03	04	05	06	07	08	09	10	11	12
SAT	01	02	03	04	05	06	07	08	09	10	11	12
SUN	01	02	03	04	05	06	07	08	09	10	11	12

NOTES:

DATE I STARTED TRACKING:

DEPRESSION Tracker

Document the days when you experienced depression. This page includes a 3-week tracker.

DEPRESSION LEVELS (1-MILD, 10 SEVERE)

Day	01	02	03	04	05	06	07	08	09	10	11	12
MON	01	02	03	04	05	06	07	08	09	10	11	12
TUE	01	02	03	04	05	06	07	08	09	10	11	12
WED	01	02	03	04	05	06	07	08	09	10	11	12
THU	01	02	03	04	05	06	07	08	09	10	11	12
FRI	01	02	03	04	05	06	07	08	09	10	11	12
SAT	01	02	03	04	05	06	07	08	09	10	11	12
SUN	01	02	03	04	05	06	07	08	09	10	11	12
MON	01	02	03	04	05	06	07	08	09	10	11	12
TUE	01	02	03	04	05	06	07	08	09	10	11	12
WED	01	02	03	04	05	06	07	08	09	10	11	12
THU	01	02	03	04	05	06	07	08	09	10	11	12
FRI	01	02	03	04	05	06	07	08	09	10	11	12
SAT	01	02	03	04	05	06	07	08	09	10	11	12
SUN	01	02	03	04	05	06	07	08	09	10	11	12
MON	01	02	03	04	05	06	07	08	09	10	11	12
TUE	01	02	03	04	05	06	07	08	09	10	11	12
WED	01	02	03	04	05	06	07	08	09	10	11	12
THU	01	02	03	04	05	06	07	08	09	10	11	12
FRI	01	02	03	04	05	06	07	08	09	10	11	12
SAT	01	02	03	04	05	06	07	08	09	10	11	12
SUN	01	02	03	04	05	06	07	08	09	10	11	12

NOTES:

DATE I STARTED TRACKING:

RESET *your mind*

We can't always control the way our thoughts but we can learn to transform negative feelings into positive ones and control our reactions and impulses. Use the chart below to start the process.

WHEN I FEEL LIKE:		I WILL TRY TO CONTROL BY REACTIONS BY:
	}	
	}	
	}	
	}	
	}	
	}	
	}	
	}	
	}	
	}	
	}	
	}	
	}	

NOTES & REFLECTIONS

DOODLES & SCRIBBLES

LOVE Yourself

STEP 1: MAKE YOURSELF A PRIORITY

It's important to always put yourself first by listening to your inner voice. Let it guide you in eliminating toxic people and negative sources. Don't be afraid to distance yourself from people and places that make you feel unhappy or who don't support your journey.

STEP 2: FACE YOUR FEARS

Don't be afraid to confront your fears and self-doubt. Why do you feel unworthy at times? What are you most worried about?

STEP 3: BE ACCOUNTABLE

Hold yourself accountable for the things you can control and change. There are things in your life only you can change.

STEP 4: FORGIVE YOURSELF

Let go of past mistakes – you can't go back in time. We all have regrets and while it's important to hold yourself accountable for mistakes, you can only truly heal when you learn to forgive yourself. Free your mind so it can focus on a better you and a happier tomorrow.

STEP 5: ACCEPT WHERE YOU ARE IN YOUR JOURNEY

Don't allow yourself to grow frustrated that you aren't able to race towards the finish line. Your journey will take time so give yourself permission to fail while also learning to accept where you are right now. Take it one day at a time. You owe it to yourself to stay focused on the road ahead while celebrating every milestone along the way.

Write down your thoughts, reflections and ideas below:

Thoughts

SELF CARE *Focus*

TOP 3 SELF-CARE ACTIVITIES

1.
2.
3.

HOW THEY MAKE ME FEEL

OTHER SELF-CARE ACTIVITIES THAT MAKE ME HAPPY

01

02

03

FAVORITE QUOTES/WORDS OF ENCOURAGEMENT

TRIGGER *Sources*

Discover what causes emotional pain and negative thoughts in your life.

Describe the negative reaction/response you would like to overcome:

Consider the aspects of your life below and write down how each category can cause the above trigger.

PERSONAL

PEOPLE

PLACES

SITUATIONS

Think about the different ways you can overcome your triggers when dealing with each category.
How can you better control your reactions and manage frustrating situations?

HAPPINESS Tracker

Keep track of how often you feel happy and calm and what you did to minimize negative responses.

DATE:

HAPPINESS RATING: ☆☆☆☆☆

DATE:

HAPPINESS RATING: ☆☆☆☆☆

DATE:

HAPPINESS RATING: ☆☆☆☆☆

DATE:

HAPPINESS RATING: ☆☆☆☆☆

DATE:

HAPPINESS RATING: ☆☆☆☆☆

DATE:

HAPPINESS RATING: ☆☆☆☆☆

DATE:

DAILY Reflection

HOW I FEEL TODAY

MY GREATEST CHALLENGE

MOOD TRACKER:

MORNING:

EVENING:

I FELT HAPPY WHEN:

I FELT EXCITED WHEN:

I FELT ENERGIZED WHEN:

Today's Highlights

What I'm Grateful For Today

DAILY Awareness

MONTH:

M T W T F S S

HOW I'M FEELING TODAY

3 WORDS TO DESCRIBE MY DAY

STRUGGLES

HIGHLIGHT OF MY DAY

DAILY ACCOMPLISHMENTS

DAILY *Reflection*

DATE:

HOW I FEEL TODAY

MY GREATEST CHALLENGE

MOOD TRACKER:

MORNING:

EVENING:

I FELT HAPPY WHEN:

I FELT EXCITED WHEN:

I FELT ENERGIZED WHEN:

Today's Highlights

What I'm Grateful For Today

DAILY *Awareness*

MONTH:

M T W T F S S

HOW I'M FEELING TODAY

3 WORDS TO DESCRIBE MY DAY

STRUGGLES

HIGHLIGHT OF MY DAY

DAILY ACCOMPLISHMENTS

DAILY *Reflection*

DATE:

HOW I FEEL TODAY

MY GREATEST CHALLENGE

MOOD TRACKER:

MORNING:

EVENING:

I FELT HAPPY WHEN:

I FELT EXCITED WHEN:

I FELT ENERGIZED WHEN:

Today's Highlights

What I'm Grateful For Today

DAILY *Awareness*

MONTH:

M T W T F S S

HOW I'M FEELING TODAY

3 WORDS TO DESCRIBE MY DAY

STRUGGLES

HIGHLIGHT OF MY DAY

DAILY ACCOMPLISHMENTS

DAILY Reflection

DATE:

HOW I FEEL TODAY

MY GREATEST CHALLENGE

MOOD TRACKER:

MORNING:

EVENING:

I FELT HAPPY WHEN:

I FELT EXCITED WHEN:

I FELT ENERGIZED WHEN:

Today's Highlights

What I'm Grateful For Today

DAILY *Awareness*

MONTH:

M T W T F S S

HOW I'M FEELING TODAY

3 WORDS TO DESCRIBE MY DAY

STRUGGLES

HIGHLIGHT OF MY DAY

DAILY ACCOMPLISHMENTS

DAILY *Reflection*

DATE:

HOW I FEEL TODAY

MY GREATEST CHALLENGE

MOOD TRACKER:

MORNING:

EVENING:

I FELT HAPPY WHEN:

I FELT EXCITED WHEN:

I FELT ENERGIZED WHEN:

Today's Highlights

What I'm Grateful For Today

DAILY *Awareness*

MONTH:

M T W T F S S

HOW I'M FEELING TODAY

3 WORDS TO DESCRIBE MY DAY

STRUGGLES

HIGHLIGHT OF MY DAY

DAILY ACCOMPLISHMENTS

DATE:

DAILY Reflection

HOW I FEEL TODAY

MY GREATEST CHALLENGE

MOOD TRACKER:

MORNING:

EVENING:

I FELT HAPPY WHEN:

I FELT EXCITED WHEN:

I FELT ENERGIZED WHEN:

Today's Highlights

What I'm Grateful For Today

DAILY *Awareness*

MONTH:

M T W T F S S

HOW I'M FEELING TODAY

3 WORDS TO DESCRIBE MY DAY

STRUGGLES

HIGHLIGHT OF MY DAY

DAILY ACCOMPLISHMENTS

DAILY *Reflection*

DATE:

HOW I FEEL TODAY

MY GREATEST CHALLENGE

MOOD TRACKER:

MORNING:

EVENING:

I FELT HAPPY WHEN:

I FELT EXCITED WHEN:

I FELT ENERGIZED WHEN:

Today's Highlights

What I'm Grateful For Today

DAILY *Awareness*

MONTH:

M T W T F S S

HOW I'M FEELING TODAY

3 WORDS TO DESCRIBE MY DAY

STRUGGLES

HIGHLIGHT OF MY DAY

DAILY ACCOMPLISHMENTS

POST Therapy Chart

DATE:

SUMMARY/OVERVIEW OF THERAPY SESSION

WHAT WE DISCUSSED

HOW IT MADE ME FEEL

WHAT I LEARNED

WHAT I WANT TO DISCUSS NEXT

Rate your session to keep track of progress.

SESSION SCORE

WEEKLY *Assessment*

	SLEEP	MOOD	POSITIVES	NEGATIVES
MONDAY				
TUESDAY				
WEDNESDAY				
THURSDAY				
FRIDAY				
SATURADY				
SUNDAY				

WEEKLY *Reflections*

Monday

Tuesday

Wednesday

Thursday

Friday

Saturday

Sunday

DATE:

DAILY *Reflection*

HOW I FEEL TODAY　　　　　　　　　　　　**MY GREATEST CHALLENGE**

MOOD TRACKER:

MORNING:　　　　　　　　　　　　EVENING:

I FELT HAPPY WHEN:　　　**I FELT EXCITED WHEN:**　　　**I FELT ENERGIZED WHEN:**

Today's Highlights

What I'm Grateful For Today

DAILY *Awareness*

MONTH:

M T W T F S S
☐ ☐ ☐ ☐ ☐ ☐ ☐

HOW I'M FEELING TODAY

3 WORDS TO DESCRIBE MY DAY

STRUGGLES

HIGHLIGHT OF MY DAY

DAILY ACCOMPLISHMENTS

DATE:

DAILY *Reflection*

HOW I FEEL TODAY   **MY GREATEST CHALLENGE**

MOOD TRACKER:

MORNING: EVENING:

I FELT HAPPY WHEN: I FELT EXCITED WHEN: I FELT ENERGIZED WHEN:

Today's Highlights

What I'm Grateful For Today

DAILY Awareness

MONTH:

M T W T F S S
☐ ☐ ☐ ☐ ☐ ☐ ☐

HOW I'M FEELING TODAY

3 WORDS TO DESCRIBE MY DAY

STRUGGLES

HIGHLIGHT OF MY DAY

DAILY ACCOMPLISHMENTS

DATE:

DAILY *Reflection*

HOW I FEEL TODAY

MY GREATEST CHALLENGE

MOOD TRACKER:

MORNING:

EVENING:

I FELT HAPPY WHEN:

I FELT EXCITED WHEN:

I FELT ENERGIZED WHEN:

Today's Highlights

What I'm Grateful For Today

DAILY *Awareness*

MONTH:

M T W T F S S
☐ ☐ ☐ ☐ ☐ ☐ ☐

HOW I'M FEELING TODAY

3 WORDS TO DESCRIBE MY DAY

STRUGGLES

HIGHLIGHT OF MY DAY

DAILY ACCOMPLISHMENTS

DATE:

DAILY *Reflection*

HOW I FEEL TODAY **MY GREATEST CHALLENGE**

MOOD TRACKER:

MORNING: EVENING:

I FELT HAPPY WHEN: **I FELT EXCITED WHEN:** **I FELT ENERGIZED WHEN:**

Today's Highlights

What I'm Grateful For Today

DAILY *Awareness*

MONTH:

M T W T F S S
☐ ☐ ☐ ☐ ☐ ☐ ☐

HOW I'M FEELING TODAY

3 WORDS TO DESCRIBE MY DAY

STRUGGLES

HIGHLIGHT OF MY DAY

DAILY ACCOMPLISHMENTS

DATE:

DAILY Reflection

HOW I FEEL TODAY **MY GREATEST CHALLENGE**

MOOD TRACKER:

MORNING: **EVENING:**

I FELT HAPPY WHEN: **I FELT EXCITED WHEN:** **I FELT ENERGIZED WHEN:**

Today's Highlights

What I'm Grateful For Today

DAILY *Awareness*

MONTH:

M T W T F S S
☐ ☐ ☐ ☐ ☐ ☐ ☐

HOW I'M FEELING TODAY

3 WORDS TO DESCRIBE MY DAY

STRUGGLES

HIGHLIGHT OF MY DAY

DAILY ACCOMPLISHMENTS

DATE:

DAILY Reflection

HOW I FEEL TODAY **MY GREATEST CHALLENGE**

MOOD TRACKER:

MORNING: EVENING:

I FELT HAPPY WHEN: I FELT EXCITED WHEN: I FELT ENERGIZED WHEN:

Today's Highlights

What I'm Grateful For Today

DAILY Awareness

MONTH:

M T W T F S S
☐ ☐ ☐ ☐ ☐ ☐ ☐

HOW I'M FEELING TODAY

3 WORDS TO DESCRIBE MY DAY

STRUGGLES

HIGHLIGHT OF MY DAY

DAILY ACCOMPLISHMENTS

DATE:

DAILY *Reflection*

HOW I FEEL TODAY **MY GREATEST CHALLENGE**

MOOD TRACKER:

MORNING: **EVENING:**

I FELT HAPPY WHEN: **I FELT EXCITED WHEN:** **I FELT ENERGIZED WHEN:**

Today's Highlights

What I'm Grateful For Today

DAILY Awareness

MONTH:

M T W T F S S
☐ ☐ ☐ ☐ ☐ ☐ ☐

HOW I'M FEELING TODAY

3 WORDS TO DESCRIBE MY DAY

STRUGGLES

HIGHLIGHT OF MY DAY

DAILY ACCOMPLISHMENTS

POST Therapy Chart

DATE:

SUMMARY/OVERVIEW OF THERAPY SESSION

WHAT WE DISCUSSED

HOW IT MADE ME FEEL

WHAT I LEARNED

WHAT I WANT TO DISCUSS NEXT

Rate your session to keep track of progress.

SESSION SCORE

WEEKLY *Assessment*

	SLEEP	MOOD	POSITIVES	NEGATIVES
MONDAY				
TUESDAY				
WEDNESDAY				
THURSDAY				
FRIDAY				
SATURDAY				
SUNDAY				

WEEKLY *Reflections*

Monday

Tuesday

Wednesday

Thursday

Friday

Saturday

Sunday

DAILY Reflection

DATE:

HOW I FEEL TODAY

MY GREATEST CHALLENGE

MOOD TRACKER:

MORNING:

EVENING:

I FELT HAPPY WHEN:

I FELT EXCITED WHEN:

I FELT ENERGIZED WHEN:

Today's Highlights

What I'm Grateful For Today

DAILY Awareness

MONTH:

M T W T F S S

HOW I'M FEELING TODAY

3 WORDS TO DESCRIBE MY DAY

STRUGGLES

HIGHLIGHT OF MY DAY

DAILY ACCOMPLISHMENTS

DAILY *Reflection*

DATE:

HOW I FEEL TODAY

MY GREATEST CHALLENGE

MOOD TRACKER:

MORNING:

EVENING:

I FELT HAPPY WHEN:

I FELT EXCITED WHEN:

I FELT ENERGIZED WHEN:

Today's Highlights

What I'm Grateful For Today

DAILY Awareness

MONTH:

M T W T F S S

HOW I'M FEELING TODAY

3 WORDS TO DESCRIBE MY DAY

STRUGGLES

HIGHLIGHT OF MY DAY

DAILY ACCOMPLISHMENTS

DATE:

DAILY Reflection

HOW I FEEL TODAY

MY GREATEST CHALLENGE

MOOD TRACKER:

MORNING:

EVENING:

I FELT HAPPY WHEN:

I FELT EXCITED WHEN:

I FELT ENERGIZED WHEN:

Today's Highlights

What I'm Grateful For Today

DAILY *Awareness*

MONTH:

M T W T F S S

HOW I'M FEELING TODAY

3 WORDS TO DESCRIBE MY DAY

STRUGGLES

HIGHLIGHT OF MY DAY

DAILY ACCOMPLISHMENTS

DAILY *Reflection*

DATE:

HOW I FEEL TODAY

MY GREATEST CHALLENGE

MOOD TRACKER:

MORNING:

EVENING:

I FELT HAPPY WHEN:

I FELT EXCITED WHEN:

I FELT ENERGIZED WHEN:

Today's Highlights

What I'm Grateful For Today

DAILY Awareness

MONTH:

M T W T F S S

HOW I'M FEELING TODAY

3 WORDS TO DESCRIBE MY DAY

STRUGGLES

HIGHLIGHT OF MY DAY

DAILY ACCOMPLISHMENTS

DATE:

DAILY Reflection

HOW I FEEL TODAY

MY GREATEST CHALLENGE

MOOD TRACKER:

MORNING:

EVENING:

I FELT HAPPY WHEN:

I FELT EXCITED WHEN:

I FELT ENERGIZED WHEN:

Today's Highlights

What I'm Grateful For Today

DAILY *Awareness*

MONTH:

M T W T F S S

HOW I'M FEELING TODAY

3 WORDS TO DESCRIBE MY DAY　　　　　　　　**STRUGGLES**

HIGHLIGHT OF MY DAY

DAILY ACCOMPLISHMENTS

DATE:

DAILY Reflection

HOW I FEEL TODAY

MY GREATEST CHALLENGE

MOOD TRACKER:

MORNING:

EVENING:

I FELT HAPPY WHEN:

I FELT EXCITED WHEN:

I FELT ENERGIZED WHEN:

Today's Highlights

What I'm Grateful For Today

DAILY *Awareness*

MONTH:

M T W T F S S

HOW I'M FEELING TODAY

3 WORDS TO DESCRIBE MY DAY

STRUGGLES

HIGHLIGHT OF MY DAY

DAILY ACCOMPLISHMENTS

DAILY Reflection

DATE:

HOW I FEEL TODAY

MY GREATEST CHALLENGE

MOOD TRACKER:

MORNING:

EVENING:

I FELT HAPPY WHEN:

I FELT EXCITED WHEN:

I FELT ENERGIZED WHEN:

Today's Highlights

What I'm Grateful For Today

ANXIETY Tracker

Document the days when you experienced anxiety. This page includes a 3-week tracker.

ANXIETY LEVELS (1-MILD, 10 SEVERE)

Day													Notes
MON	01	02	03	04	05	06	07	08	09	10	11	12	**NOTES:**
TUE	01	02	03	04	05	06	07	08	09	10	11	12	
WED	01	02	03	04	05	06	07	08	09	10	11	12	
THU	01	02	03	04	05	06	07	08	09	10	11	12	
FRI	01	02	03	04	05	06	07	08	09	10	11	12	
SAT	01	02	03	04	05	06	07	08	09	10	11	12	
SUN	01	02	03	04	05	06	07	08	09	10	11	12	
MON	01	02	03	04	05	06	07	08	09	10	11	12	
TUE	01	02	03	04	05	06	07	08	09	10	11	12	
WED	01	02	03	04	05	06	07	08	09	10	11	12	
THU	01	02	03	04	05	06	07	08	09	10	11	12	
FRI	01	02	03	04	05	06	07	08	09	10	11	12	
SAT	01	02	03	04	05	06	07	08	09	10	11	12	
SUN	01	02	03	04	05	06	07	08	09	10	11	12	
MON	01	02	03	04	05	06	07	08	09	10	11	12	
TUE	01	02	03	04	05	06	07	08	09	10	11	12	
WED	01	02	03	04	05	06	07	08	09	10	11	12	
THU	01	02	03	04	05	06	07	08	09	10	11	12	
FRI	01	02	03	04	05	06	07	08	09	10	11	12	
SAT	01	02	03	04	05	06	07	08	09	10	11	12	
SUN	01	02	03	04	05	06	07	08	09	10	11	12	

DATE I STARTED TRACKING:

DEPRESSION *Tracker*

Document the days when you experienced depression. This page includes a 3-week tracker.

DEPRESSION LEVELS (1-MILD, 10 SEVERE)

Day												
MON	01	02	03	04	05	06	07	08	09	10	11	12
TUE	01	02	03	04	05	06	07	08	09	10	11	12
WED	01	02	03	04	05	06	07	08	09	10	11	12
THU	01	02	03	04	05	06	07	08	09	10	11	12
FRI	01	02	03	04	05	06	07	08	09	10	11	12
SAT	01	02	03	04	05	06	07	08	09	10	11	12
SUN	01	02	03	04	05	06	07	08	09	10	11	12
MON	01	02	03	04	05	06	07	08	09	10	11	12
TUE	01	02	03	04	05	06	07	08	09	10	11	12
WED	01	02	03	04	05	06	07	08	09	10	11	12
THU	01	02	03	04	05	06	07	08	09	10	11	12
FRI	01	02	03	04	05	06	07	08	09	10	11	12
SAT	01	02	03	04	05	06	07	08	09	10	11	12
SUN	01	02	03	04	05	06	07	08	09	10	11	12
MON	01	02	03	04	05	06	07	08	09	10	11	12
TUE	01	02	03	04	05	06	07	08	09	10	11	12
WED	01	02	03	04	05	06	07	08	09	10	11	12
THU	01	02	03	04	05	06	07	08	09	10	11	12
FRI	01	02	03	04	05	06	07	08	09	10	11	12
SAT	01	02	03	04	05	06	07	08	09	10	11	12
SUN	01	02	03	04	05	06	07	08	09	10	11	12

NOTES:

DATE I STARTED TRACKING:

DAILY *Awareness*

MONTH:

M T W T F S S

HOW I'M FEELING TODAY

3 WORDS TO DESCRIBE MY DAY

STRUGGLES

HIGHLIGHT OF MY DAY

DAILY ACCOMPLISHMENTS

POST Therapy Chart

DATE:

SUMMARY/OVERVIEW OF THERAPY SESSION

WHAT WE DISCUSSED

HOW IT MADE ME FEEL

WHAT I LEARNED

WHAT I WANT TO DISCUSS NEXT

Rate your session to keep track of progress.

SESSION SCORE

THOUGHTS *Tracker*

MONITORING YOUR THOUGHTS & FEELINGS

MONDAY'S THOUGHTS

TUESDAY'S THOUGHTS

WEDNESDAY'S THOUGHTS

THURSDAY'S THOUGHTS

FRIDAY'S THOUGHTS

SATURDAY'S THOUGHTS

SUNDAY'S THOUGHTS

WEEKLY Assessment

	SLEEP	MOOD	POSITIVES	NEGATIVES
MONDAY				
TUESDAY				
WEDNESDAY				
THURSDAY				
FRIDAY				
SATURDAY				
SUNDAY				

WEEKLY *Reflections*

Monday

Tuesday

Wednesday

Thursday

Friday

Saturday

Sunday

DAILY Reflection

DATE:

HOW I FEEL TODAY

MY GREATEST CHALLENGE

MOOD TRACKER:

MORNING:

EVENING:

I FELT HAPPY WHEN:

I FELT EXCITED WHEN:

I FELT ENERGIZED WHEN:

Today's Highlights

What I'm Grateful For Today

DAILY Awareness

MONTH:

M T W T F S S

HOW I'M FEELING TODAY

3 WORDS TO DESCRIBE MY DAY

STRUGGLES

HIGHLIGHT OF MY DAY

DAILY ACCOMPLISHMENTS

DATE:

DAILY *Reflection*

HOW I FEEL TODAY

MY GREATEST CHALLENGE

MOOD TRACKER:

MORNING:

EVENING:

I FELT HAPPY WHEN:

I FELT EXCITED WHEN:

I FELT ENERGIZED WHEN:

Today's Highlights

What I'm Grateful For Today

DAILY *Awareness*

MONTH:

M T W T F S S

HOW I'M FEELING TODAY

3 WORDS TO DESCRIBE MY DAY

STRUGGLES

HIGHLIGHT OF MY DAY

DAILY ACCOMPLISHMENTS

DATE:

DAILY Reflection

HOW I FEEL TODAY

MY GREATEST CHALLENGE

MOOD TRACKER:

MORNING:

EVENING:

I FELT HAPPY WHEN:

I FELT EXCITED WHEN:

I FELT ENERGIZED WHEN:

Today's Highlights

What I'm Grateful For Today

DAILY *Awareness*

MONTH:

M T W T F S S

HOW I'M FEELING TODAY

3 WORDS TO DESCRIBE MY DAY

STRUGGLES

HIGHLIGHT OF MY DAY

DAILY ACCOMPLISHMENTS

DAILY *Reflection*

DATE:

HOW I FEEL TODAY

MY GREATEST CHALLENGE

MOOD TRACKER:

MORNING:

EVENING:

I FELT HAPPY WHEN:

I FELT EXCITED WHEN:

I FELT ENERGIZED WHEN:

Today's Highlights

What I'm Grateful For Today

DAILY Awareness

MONTH:

M T W T F S S

HOW I'M FEELING TODAY

3 WORDS TO DESCRIBE MY DAY

STRUGGLES

HIGHLIGHT OF MY DAY

DAILY ACCOMPLISHMENTS

DATE:

DAILY Reflection

HOW I FEEL TODAY

MY GREATEST CHALLENGE

MOOD TRACKER:

MORNING:

EVENING:

I FELT HAPPY WHEN:

I FELT EXCITED WHEN:

I FELT ENERGIZED WHEN:

Today's Highlights

What I'm Grateful For Today

DAILY *Awareness*

MONTH:

M T W T F S S

HOW I'M FEELING TODAY

3 WORDS TO DESCRIBE MY DAY

STRUGGLES

HIGHLIGHT OF MY DAY

DAILY ACCOMPLISHMENTS

DATE:

DAILY *Reflection*

HOW I FEEL TODAY

MY GREATEST CHALLENGE

MOOD TRACKER:

MORNING:

EVENING:

I FELT HAPPY WHEN:

I FELT EXCITED WHEN:

I FELT ENERGIZED WHEN:

Today's Highlights

What I'm Grateful For Today

DAILY Awareness

MONTH:

M T W T F S S

HOW I'M FEELING TODAY

3 WORDS TO DESCRIBE MY DAY

STRUGGLES

HIGHLIGHT OF MY DAY

DAILY ACCOMPLISHMENTS

DATE:

DAILY *Reflection*

HOW I FEEL TODAY

MY GREATEST CHALLENGE

MOOD TRACKER:

MORNING:

EVENING:

I FELT HAPPY WHEN:

I FELT EXCITED WHEN:

I FELT ENERGIZED WHEN:

Today's Highlights

What I'm Grateful For Today

DAILY Awareness

MONTH:

M T W T F S S

HOW I'M FEELING TODAY

3 WORDS TO DESCRIBE MY DAY

STRUGGLES

HIGHLIGHT OF MY DAY

DAILY ACCOMPLISHMENTS

POST Therapy Chart

DATE:

SUMMARY/OVERVIEW OF THERAPY SESSION

WHAT WE DISCUSSED

HOW IT MADE ME FEEL

WHAT I LEARNED

WHAT I WANT TO DISCUSS NEXT

Rate your session to keep track of progress.

SESSION SCORE

THOUGHTS *Tracker*

MONITORING YOUR THOUGHTS & FEELINGS

MONDAY'S THOUGHTS

TUESDAY'S THOUGHTS

WEDNESDAY'S THOUGHTS

THURSDAY'S THOUGHTS

FRIDAY'S THOUGHTS

SATURDAY'S THOUGHTS

SUNDAY'S THOUGHTS

WEEKLY *Assessment*

	SLEEP	MOOD	POSITIVES	NEGATIVES
MONDAY				
TUESDAY				
WEDNESDAY				
THURSDAY				
FRIDAY				
SATURADY				
SUNDAY				

WEEKLY *Reflections*

Monday

Tuesday

Wednesday

Thursday

Friday

Saturday

Sunday

DATE:

DAILY Reflection

HOW I FEEL TODAY

MY GREATEST CHALLENGE

MOOD TRACKER:

MORNING:

EVENING:

I FELT HAPPY WHEN:

I FELT EXCITED WHEN:

I FELT ENERGIZED WHEN:

Today's Highlights

What I'm Grateful For Today

DAILY Awareness

MONTH:

M T W T F S S

HOW I'M FEELING TODAY

3 WORDS TO DESCRIBE MY DAY

STRUGGLES

HIGHLIGHT OF MY DAY

DAILY ACCOMPLISHMENTS

DATE:

DAILY Reflection

HOW I FEEL TODAY

MY GREATEST CHALLENGE

MOOD TRACKER:

MORNING:

EVENING:

I FELT HAPPY WHEN:

I FELT EXCITED WHEN:

I FELT ENERGIZED WHEN:

Today's Highlights

What I'm Grateful For Today

DAILY *Awareness*

MONTH:

M T W T F S S

HOW I'M FEELING TODAY

3 WORDS TO DESCRIBE MY DAY

STRUGGLES

HIGHLIGHT OF MY DAY

DAILY ACCOMPLISHMENTS

DAILY *Reflection*

DATE:

HOW I FEEL TODAY

MY GREATEST CHALLENGE

MOOD TRACKER:

MORNING:

EVENING:

I FELT HAPPY WHEN:

I FELT EXCITED WHEN:

I FELT ENERGIZED WHEN:

Today's Highlights

What I'm Grateful For Today

DAILY Awareness

MONTH:

M T W T F S S

HOW I'M FEELING TODAY

3 WORDS TO DESCRIBE MY DAY

STRUGGLES

HIGHLIGHT OF MY DAY

DAILY ACCOMPLISHMENTS

DATE:

DAILY *Reflection*

HOW I FEEL TODAY

MY GREATEST CHALLENGE

MOOD TRACKER:

MORNING:

EVENING:

I FELT HAPPY WHEN:

I FELT EXCITED WHEN:

I FELT ENERGIZED WHEN:

Today's Highlights

What I'm Grateful For Today

DAILY *Awareness*

MONTH:

M T W T F S S

HOW I'M FEELING TODAY

3 WORDS TO DESCRIBE MY DAY

STRUGGLES

HIGHLIGHT OF MY DAY

DAILY ACCOMPLISHMENTS

DATE:

DAILY Reflection

HOW I FEEL TODAY

MY GREATEST CHALLENGE

MOOD TRACKER:

MORNING:

EVENING:

I FELT HAPPY WHEN:

I FELT EXCITED WHEN:

I FELT ENERGIZED WHEN:

Today's Highlights

What I'm Grateful For Today

DAILY Awareness

MONTH:

M T W T F S S

HOW I'M FEELING TODAY

3 WORDS TO DESCRIBE MY DAY

STRUGGLES

HIGHLIGHT OF MY DAY

DAILY ACCOMPLISHMENTS

DATE:

DAILY Reflection

HOW I FEEL TODAY

MY GREATEST CHALLENGE

MOOD TRACKER:

MORNING:

EVENING:

I FELT HAPPY WHEN:

I FELT EXCITED WHEN:

I FELT ENERGIZED WHEN:

Today's Highlights

What I'm Grateful For Today

DAILY Awareness

MONTH:

M T W T F S S

HOW I'M FEELING TODAY

3 WORDS TO DESCRIBE MY DAY

STRUGGLES

HIGHLIGHT OF MY DAY

DAILY ACCOMPLISHMENTS

DATE:

DAILY *Reflection*

HOW I FEEL TODAY

MY GREATEST CHALLENGE

MOOD TRACKER:

MORNING:

EVENING:

I FELT HAPPY WHEN:

I FELT EXCITED WHEN:

I FELT ENERGIZED WHEN:

Today's Highlights

What I'm Grateful For Today

DAILY *Awareness*

MONTH:

M T W T F S S

HOW I'M FEELING TODAY

3 WORDS TO DESCRIBE MY DAY

STRUGGLES

HIGHLIGHT OF MY DAY

DAILY ACCOMPLISHMENTS

POST Therapy Chart

DATE:

SUMMARY/OVERVIEW OF THERAPY SESSION

WHAT WE DISCUSSED

HOW IT MADE ME FEEL

WHAT I LEARNED

WHAT I WANT TO DISCUSS NEXT

Rate your session to keep track of progress.

SESSION SCORE

THOUGHTS *Tracker*

MONITORING YOUR THOUGHTS & FEELINGS

MONDAY'S THOUGHTS

TUESDAY'S THOUGHTS

WEDNESDAY'S THOUGHTS

THURSDAY'S THOUGHTS

FRIDAY'S THOUGHTS

SATURDAY'S THOUGHTS

SUNDAY'S THOUGHTS

WEEKLY Assessment

	SLEEP	MOOD	POSITIVES	NEGATIVES
MONDAY				
TUESDAY				
WEDNESDAY				
THURSDAY				
FRIDAY				
SATURDAY				
SUNDAY				

WEEKLY *Reflections*

Monday

Tuesday

Wednesday

Thursday

Friday

Saturday

Sunday

DATE:

DAILY Reflection

HOW I FEEL TODAY

MY GREATEST CHALLENGE

MOOD TRACKER:

MORNING:

EVENING:

I FELT HAPPY WHEN:

I FELT EXCITED WHEN:

I FELT ENERGIZED WHEN:

Today's Highlights

What I'm Grateful For Today

DAILY *Awareness*

MONTH:

M T W T F S S

HOW I'M FEELING TODAY

3 WORDS TO DESCRIBE MY DAY

STRUGGLES

HIGHLIGHT OF MY DAY

DAILY ACCOMPLISHMENTS

DAILY *Reflection*

DATE:

HOW I FEEL TODAY

MY GREATEST CHALLENGE

MOOD TRACKER:

MORNING:

EVENING:

I FELT HAPPY WHEN:

I FELT EXCITED WHEN:

I FELT ENERGIZED WHEN:

Today's Highlights

What I'm Grateful For Today

DAILY *Awareness*

MONTH:

M T W T F S S

HOW I'M FEELING TODAY

3 WORDS TO DESCRIBE MY DAY

STRUGGLES

HIGHLIGHT OF MY DAY

DAILY ACCOMPLISHMENTS

DAILY *Reflection*

DATE:

HOW I FEEL TODAY

MY GREATEST CHALLENGE

MOOD TRACKER:

MORNING:

EVENING:

I FELT HAPPY WHEN:

I FELT EXCITED WHEN:

I FELT ENERGIZED WHEN:

Today's Highlights

What I'm Grateful For Today

DAILY *Awareness*

MONTH:

M T W T F S S

HOW I'M FEELING TODAY

3 WORDS TO DESCRIBE MY DAY

STRUGGLES

HIGHLIGHT OF MY DAY

DAILY ACCOMPLISHMENTS

DATE:

DAILY Reflection

HOW I FEEL TODAY

MY GREATEST CHALLENGE

MOOD TRACKER:

MORNING:

EVENING:

I FELT HAPPY WHEN:

I FELT EXCITED WHEN:

I FELT ENERGIZED WHEN:

Today's Highlights

What I'm Grateful For Today

DAILY *Awareness*

MONTH:

M T W T F S S

HOW I'M FEELING TODAY

3 WORDS TO DESCRIBE MY DAY

STRUGGLES

HIGHLIGHT OF MY DAY

DAILY ACCOMPLISHMENTS

DATE:

DAILY Reflection

HOW I FEEL TODAY

MY GREATEST CHALLENGE

MOOD TRACKER:

MORNING:

EVENING:

I FELT HAPPY WHEN:

I FELT EXCITED WHEN:

I FELT ENERGIZED WHEN:

Today's Highlights

What I'm Grateful For Today

DAILY Awareness

MONTH:

M T W T F S S

HOW I'M FEELING TODAY

3 WORDS TO DESCRIBE MY DAY

STRUGGLES

HIGHLIGHT OF MY DAY

DAILY ACCOMPLISHMENTS

DATE:

DAILY Reflection

HOW I FEEL TODAY

MY GREATEST CHALLENGE

MOOD TRACKER:

MORNING:

EVENING:

I FELT HAPPY WHEN:

I FELT EXCITED WHEN:

I FELT ENERGIZED WHEN:

Today's Highlights

What I'm Grateful For Today

DAILY *Awareness*

MONTH:

M T W T F S S

HOW I'M FEELING TODAY

3 WORDS TO DESCRIBE MY DAY

STRUGGLES

HIGHLIGHT OF MY DAY

DAILY ACCOMPLISHMENTS

DAILY *Reflection*

DATE:

HOW I FEEL TODAY

MY GREATEST CHALLENGE

MOOD TRACKER:

MORNING:

EVENING:

I FELT HAPPY WHEN:

I FELT EXCITED WHEN:

I FELT ENERGIZED WHEN:

Today's Highlights

What I'm Grateful For Today

DAILY *Awareness*

MONTH:

M T W T F S S

HOW I'M FEELING TODAY

3 WORDS TO DESCRIBE MY DAY

STRUGGLES

HIGHLIGHT OF MY DAY

DAILY ACCOMPLISHMENTS

POST Therapy Chart

DATE: _____

SUMMARY/OVERVIEW OF THERAPY SESSION

WHAT WE DISCUSSED

HOW IT MADE ME FEEL

WHAT I LEARNED

WHAT I WANT TO DISCUSS NEXT

Rate your session to keep track of progress.

SESSION SCORE: __ / __

THOUGHTS *Tracker*

MONITORING YOUR THOUGHTS & FEELINGS

MONDAY'S THOUGHTS

TUESDAY'S THOUGHTS

WEDNESDAY'S THOUGHTS

THURSDAY'S THOUGHTS

FRIDAY'S THOUGHTS

SATURDAY'S THOUGHTS

SUNDAY'S THOUGHTS

WEEKLY *Reflections*

Monday

Tuesday

Wednesday

Thursday

Friday

Saturday

Sunday

DATE:

DAILY *Reflection*

HOW I FEEL TODAY   **MY GREATEST CHALLENGE**

MOOD TRACKER:

MORNING: **EVENING:**

I FELT HAPPY WHEN: **I FELT EXCITED WHEN:**   **I FELT ENERGIZED WHEN:**

Today's Highlights

What I'm Grateful For Today

DAILY Awareness

MONTH:

M T W T F S S
☐ ☐ ☐ ☐ ☐ ☐ ☐

HOW I'M FEELING TODAY

3 WORDS TO DESCRIBE MY DAY

STRUGGLES

HIGHLIGHT OF MY DAY

DAILY ACCOMPLISHMENTS

DATE:

DAILY *Reflection*

HOW I FEEL TODAY **MY GREATEST CHALLENGE**

MOOD TRACKER:

MORNING: EVENING:

I FELT HAPPY WHEN: **I FELT EXCITED WHEN:** **I FELT ENERGIZED WHEN:**

Today's Highlights

What I'm Grateful For Today

DAILY *Awareness*

MONTH:

M T W T F S S
☐ ☐ ☐ ☐ ☐ ☐ ☐

HOW I'M FEELING TODAY

3 WORDS TO DESCRIBE MY DAY

STRUGGLES

HIGHLIGHT OF MY DAY

DAILY ACCOMPLISHMENTS

DATE:

DAILY Reflection

HOW I FEEL TODAY   **MY GREATEST CHALLENGE**

MOOD TRACKER:

MORNING: EVENING:

I FELT HAPPY WHEN: I FELT EXCITED WHEN: I FELT ENERGIZED WHEN:

Today's Highlights

What I'm Grateful For Today

DAILY *Awareness*

MONTH:

M T W T F S S
☐ ☐ ☐ ☐ ☐ ☐ ☐

HOW I'M FEELING TODAY

3 WORDS TO DESCRIBE MY DAY

STRUGGLES

HIGHLIGHT OF MY DAY

DAILY ACCOMPLISHMENTS

DATE:

DAILY *Reflection*

HOW I FEEL TODAY **MY GREATEST CHALLENGE**

MOOD TRACKER:

MORNING: **EVENING:**

I FELT HAPPY WHEN: **I FELT EXCITED WHEN:** **I FELT ENERGIZED WHEN:**

Today's Highlights

What I'm Grateful For Today

DAILY *Awareness*

MONTH:

M T W T F S S
☐ ☐ ☐ ☐ ☐ ☐ ☐

HOW I'M FEELING TODAY

3 WORDS TO DESCRIBE MY DAY

STRUGGLES

HIGHLIGHT OF MY DAY

DAILY ACCOMPLISHMENTS

DATE:

DAILY *Reflection*

HOW I FEEL TODAY   **MY GREATEST CHALLENGE**

MOOD TRACKER:

MORNING: **EVENING:**

I FELT HAPPY WHEN: **I FELT EXCITED WHEN:**   **I FELT ENERGIZED WHEN:**

Today's Highlights

What I'm Grateful For Today

DAILY *Awareness*

MONTH:

M T W T F S S
☐ ☐ ☐ ☐ ☐ ☐ ☐

HOW I'M FEELING TODAY

3 WORDS TO DESCRIBE MY DAY

STRUGGLES

HIGHLIGHT OF MY DAY

DAILY ACCOMPLISHMENTS

DATE:

DAILY *Reflection*

HOW I FEEL TODAY **MY GREATEST CHALLENGE**

MOOD TRACKER:

MORNING: **EVENING:**

I FELT HAPPY WHEN: **I FELT EXCITED WHEN:** **I FELT ENERGIZED WHEN:**

Today's Highlights

What I'm Grateful For Today

DAILY *Awareness*

MONTH:

M T W T F S S
☐ ☐ ☐ ☐ ☐ ☐ ☐

HOW I'M FEELING TODAY

3 WORDS TO DESCRIBE MY DAY

STRUGGLES

HIGHLIGHT OF MY DAY

DAILY ACCOMPLISHMENTS

DATE:

DAILY *Reflection*

HOW I FEEL TODAY **MY GREATEST CHALLENGE**

MOOD TRACKER:

MORNING: **EVENING:**

I FELT HAPPY WHEN: **I FELT EXCITED WHEN:** **I FELT ENERGIZED WHEN:**

Today's Highlights

What I'm Grateful For Today

DAILY Awareness

MONTH:

M T W T F S S
☐ ☐ ☐ ☐ ☐ ☐ ☐

HOW I'M FEELING TODAY

3 WORDS TO DESCRIBE MY DAY

STRUGGLES

HIGHLIGHT OF MY DAY

DAILY ACCOMPLISHMENTS

POST Therapy Chart

DATE:

SUMMARY/OVERVIEW OF THERAPY SESSION

WHAT WE DISCUSSED

HOW IT MADE ME FEEL

WHAT I LEARNED

WHAT I WANT TO DISCUSS NEXT

Rate your session to keep track of progress.

SESSION SCORE

THOUGHTS *Tracker*

MONITORING YOUR THOUGHTS & FEELINGS

MONDAY'S THOUGHTS

TUESDAY'S THOUGHTS

WEDNESDAY'S THOUGHTS

THURSDAY'S THOUGHTS

FRIDAY'S THOUGHTS

SATURDAY'S THOUGHTS

SUNDAY'S THOUGHTS

WEEKLY *Reflections*

Monday

Tuesday

Wednesday

Thursday

Friday

Saturday

Sunday

DATE:

DAILY *Reflection*

HOW I FEEL TODAY

MY GREATEST CHALLENGE

MOOD TRACKER:

MORNING:

EVENING:

I FELT HAPPY WHEN:

I FELT EXCITED WHEN:

I FELT ENERGIZED WHEN:

Today's Highlights

What I'm Grateful For Today

DAILY Awareness

MONTH:

M T W T F S S

HOW I'M FEELING TODAY

3 WORDS TO DESCRIBE MY DAY

STRUGGLES

HIGHLIGHT OF MY DAY

DAILY ACCOMPLISHMENTS

DATE:

DAILY Reflection

HOW I FEEL TODAY

MY GREATEST CHALLENGE

MOOD TRACKER:

MORNING:

EVENING:

I FELT HAPPY WHEN:

I FELT EXCITED WHEN:

I FELT ENERGIZED WHEN:

Today's Highlights

What I'm Grateful For Today

DAILY *Awareness*

MONTH:

M T W T F S S

HOW I'M FEELING TODAY

3 WORDS TO DESCRIBE MY DAY

STRUGGLES

HIGHLIGHT OF MY DAY

DAILY ACCOMPLISHMENTS

DATE:

DAILY Reflection

HOW I FEEL TODAY

MY GREATEST CHALLENGE

MOOD TRACKER:

MORNING:

EVENING:

I FELT HAPPY WHEN:

I FELT EXCITED WHEN:

I FELT ENERGIZED WHEN:

Today's Highlights

What I'm Grateful For Today

DAILY *Awareness*

MONTH:

M T W T F S S

HOW I'M FEELING TODAY

3 WORDS TO DESCRIBE MY DAY

STRUGGLES

HIGHLIGHT OF MY DAY

DAILY ACCOMPLISHMENTS

DATE:

DAILY Reflection

HOW I FEEL TODAY

MY GREATEST CHALLENGE

MOOD TRACKER:

MORNING:

EVENING:

I FELT HAPPY WHEN:

I FELT EXCITED WHEN:

I FELT ENERGIZED WHEN:

Today's Highlights

What I'm Grateful For Today

DAILY *Awareness*

MONTH:

M T W T F S S

HOW I'M FEELING TODAY

3 WORDS TO DESCRIBE MY DAY

STRUGGLES

HIGHLIGHT OF MY DAY

DAILY ACCOMPLISHMENTS

DATE:

DAILY Reflection

HOW I FEEL TODAY

MY GREATEST CHALLENGE

MOOD TRACKER:

MORNING:

EVENING:

I FELT HAPPY WHEN:

I FELT EXCITED WHEN:

I FELT ENERGIZED WHEN:

Today's Highlights

What I'm Grateful For Today

DAILY *Awareness*

MONTH:

M T W T F S S

HOW I'M FEELING TODAY

3 WORDS TO DESCRIBE MY DAY

STRUGGLES

HIGHLIGHT OF MY DAY

DAILY ACCOMPLISHMENTS

DAILY *Reflection*

DATE:

HOW I FEEL TODAY

MY GREATEST CHALLENGE

MOOD TRACKER:

MORNING:

EVENING:

I FELT HAPPY WHEN:

I FELT EXCITED WHEN:

I FELT ENERGIZED WHEN:

Today's Highlights

What I'm Grateful For Today

DAILY *Awareness*

MONTH:

M T W T F S S

HOW I'M FEELING TODAY

3 WORDS TO DESCRIBE MY DAY

STRUGGLES

HIGHLIGHT OF MY DAY

DAILY ACCOMPLISHMENTS

DATE:

DAILY Reflection

HOW I FEEL TODAY

MY GREATEST CHALLENGE

MOOD TRACKER:

MORNING:

EVENING:

I FELT HAPPY WHEN:

I FELT EXCITED WHEN:

I FELT ENERGIZED WHEN:

Today's Highlights

What I'm Grateful For Today

DAILY Awareness

MONTH:

M T W T F S S

HOW I'M FEELING TODAY

3 WORDS TO DESCRIBE MY DAY

STRUGGLES

HIGHLIGHT OF MY DAY

DAILY ACCOMPLISHMENTS

POST Therapy Chart

DATE:

SUMMARY/OVERVIEW OF THERAPY SESSION

WHAT WE DISCUSSED

HOW IT MADE ME FEEL

WHAT I LEARNED

WHAT I WANT TO DISCUSS NEXT

Rate your session to keep track of progress.

SESSION SCORE

THOUGHTS *Tracker*

MONITORING YOUR THOUGHTS & FEELINGS

MONDAY'S THOUGHTS

TUESDAY'S THOUGHTS

WEDNESDAY'S THOUGHTS

THURSDAY'S THOUGHTS

FRIDAY'S THOUGHTS

SATURDAY'S THOUGHTS

SUNDAY'S THOUGHTS

WEEKLY *Reflections*

Monday

Tuesday

Wednesday

Thursday

Friday

Saturday

Sunday

Printed in Great Britain
by Amazon